DRAWING WITH Sports Illustrated KIDS

PICTURE A SLAM DUNK

A Basketball Drawing Book

by Anthony Wacholtz   illustrated by Erwin Haya

CAPSTONE PRESS
a capstone imprint

TABLE OF CONTENTS

Step Back and Drain the Three (on Paper!)

It's time to lace up your shoes, step onto the court, and start drawing! Learn some tips and get ready to draw yourself into the action on the basketball court. Are you ready to drive the lane for a spectacular dunk? Or would you rather fire a bounce pass between defenders? What's more exciting than draining the game-winning basket at the buzzer? If you can't decide, draw them all!

Follow the simple step-by-step drawings in this book, and you'll be on your way to basketball stardom. Before you know it, you'll be part of the game. Let's get started!

Before you head out on the court, grab some supplies:

1. First you'll need drawing paper. Any type of blank, unlined paper will do.

2. Pencils are the easiest to use for your drawing projects. Make sure you have plenty of them.

3. It's easier to make clean lines with sharpened pencils. Keep a pencil sharpener close by.

4. As you practice drawing, you'll need a good eraser. Pencil erasers wear out very quickly. Get a rubber or kneaded eraser.

5. When your drawing is finished, you can trace over it with a black ink pen or a thin felt-tip marker. The dark lines will make your drawing jump off the page.

6. If you decide to color your drawings, colored pencils and markers usually work best. You can also use colored pencils to shade your drawings and make them more lifelike.

PULL-UP JUMPER

The point guard passes the ball to you on the perimeter. The ball leaves your hands, soaring over the defender's outstretched arm. Swish!

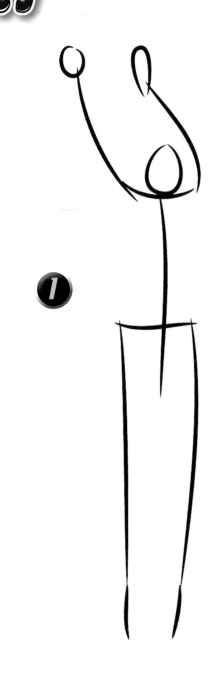

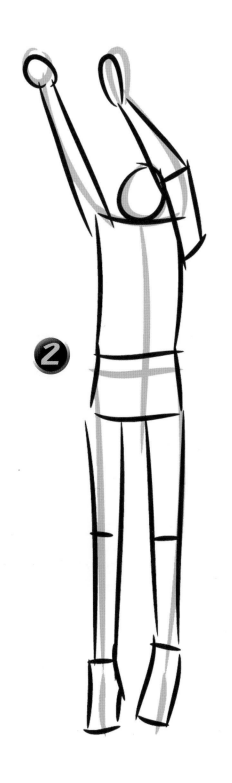

LAY IT UP

Fast break! There's nothing but open space between you and the hoop. You float gracefully toward the basket and lay it in for an easy two.

1

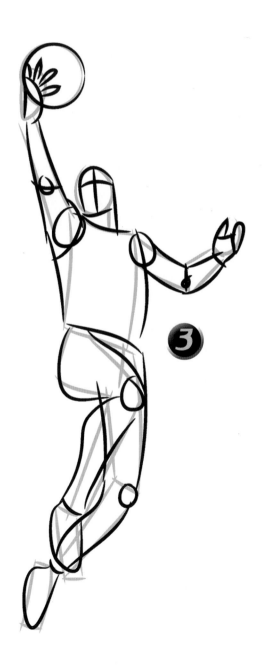

FADEAWAY

Your defender has played tight defense on you all game. You'll need some space to get a shot off. You fake forward and then jump back for a fadeaway shot. Nothing but net!

1

HANG TIME

You receive a fast-break pass from your teammate. Time to put on a show! You leap up with the ball cradled in the palm of your hand. What a dunk!

SLAM DUNK

Ready for takeoff! As you hit the peak of your jump, you bring your arms above your head. With both hands on the ball, you're set to jam the ball through the hoop.

1

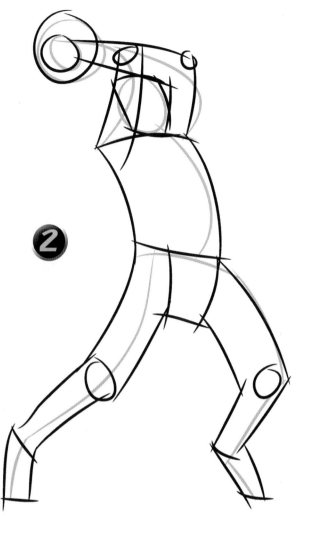

2

3

Hangin' on the Rim

A powerful dunk adds two points for your team. You hold on to the rim for a split second longer, taking in the breathtaking slam. Let's see that on a replay!

1

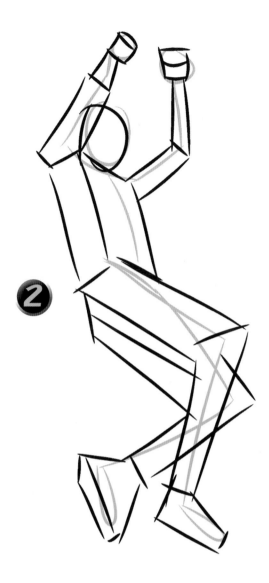

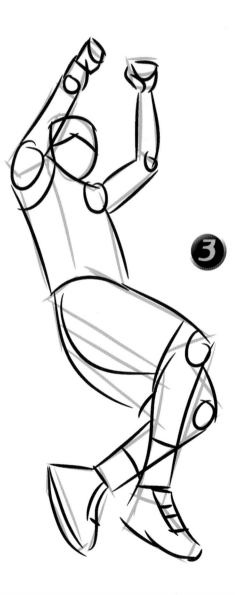

ALLEY-OOP

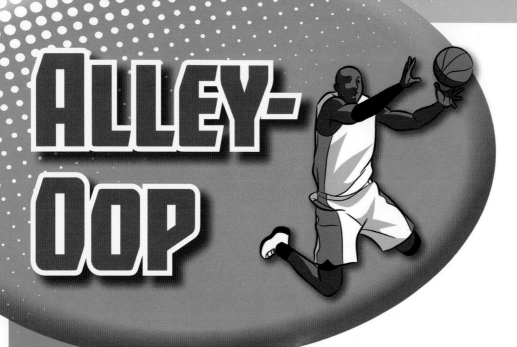

You make a break for the basket, and the point guard sees you take off. He hoists a pass toward the hoop, and you snag it in midair. You bring your arms around for a slam dunk, finishing off a perfect alley-oop.

1

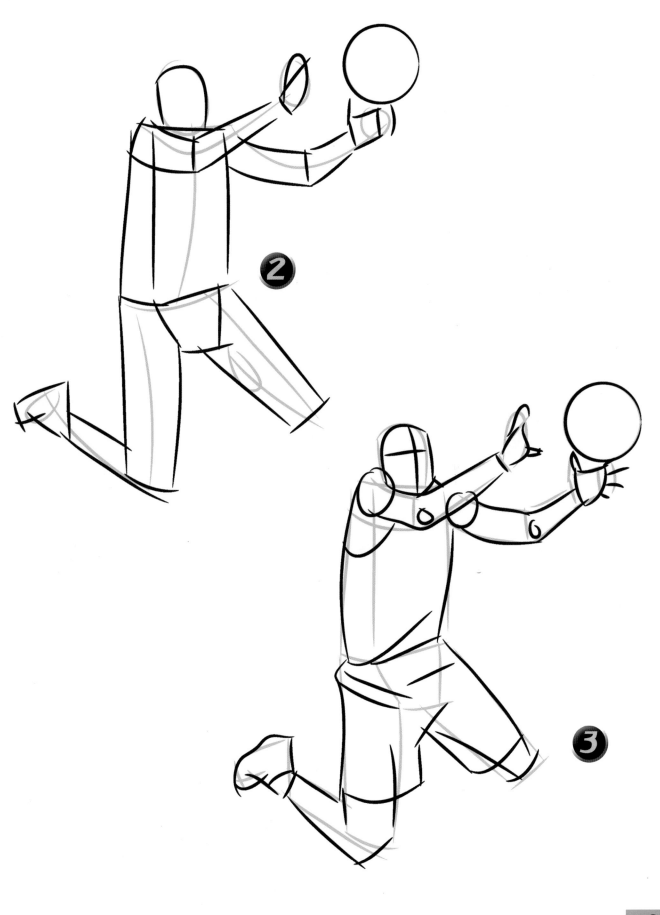

BALL CONTROL

You are the point guard—the offense is yours to command. You dribble along the perimeter, keeping your eyes peeled for an open teammate.

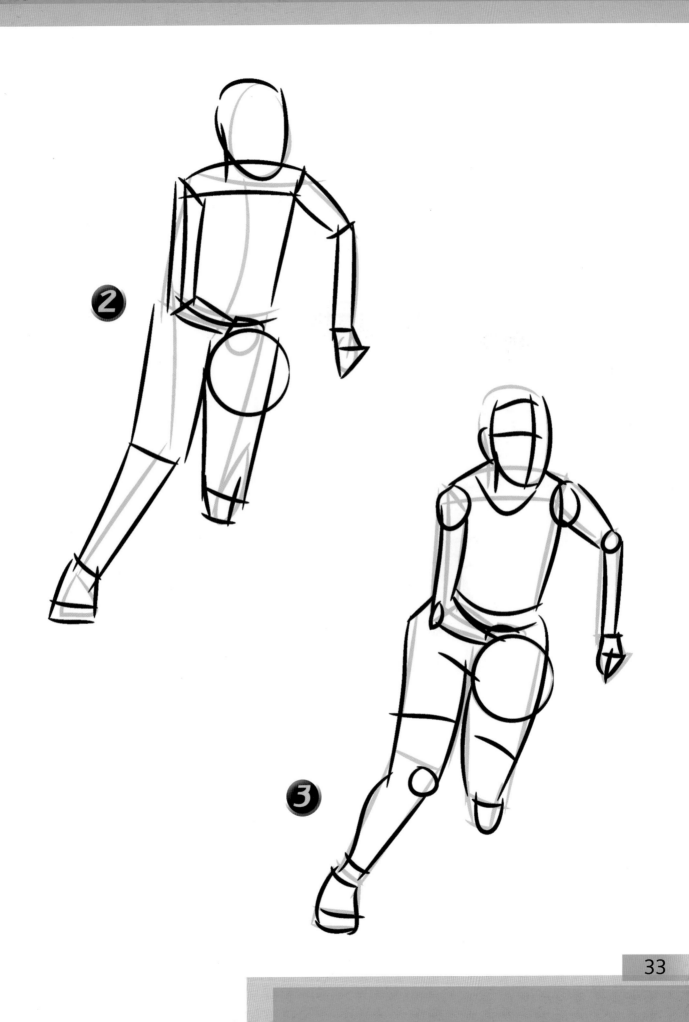

MIDAIR SAVE

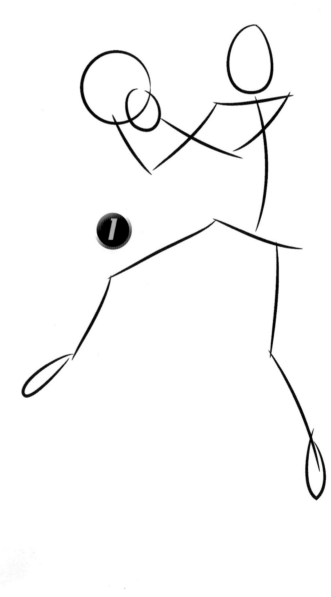

The ball bounces off a teammate's hand and toward the sideline. Not so fast! You jump toward the crowd while grabbing the ball. In the blink of an eye, you turn and fire a pass to a teammate. What a save!

⑤

DRIVING TO THE HOOP

No one's in the paint, so you decide to make your move. You catch the defender off guard, blowing by him as you drive to the hoop. They'll have to double-team you next time!

1

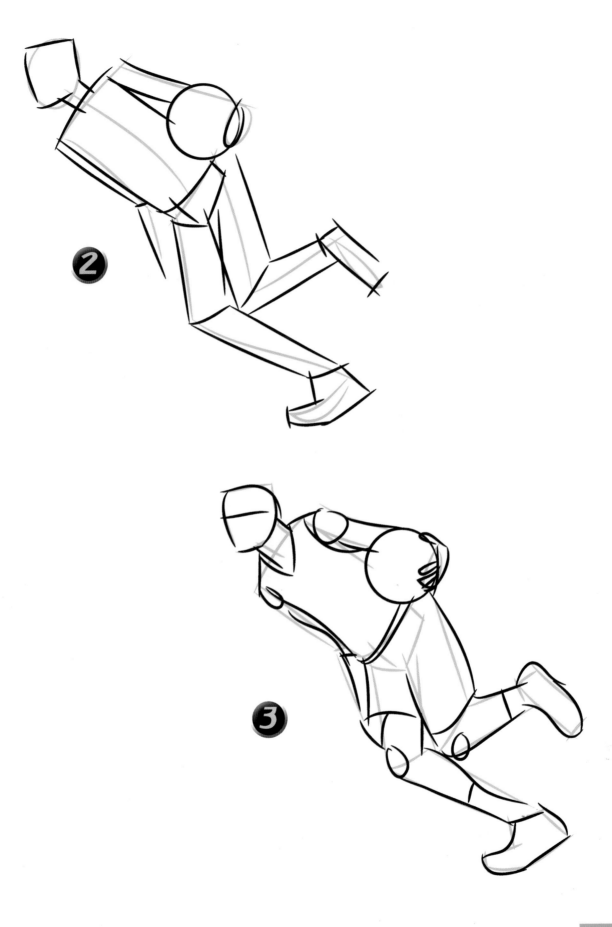

NO-LOOK PASS

You bring the ball up the court as your teammates start the play. You keep your eyes forward as a teammate breaks to the left. You send him a no-look pass—the other team never saw it coming!

DISH IT OFF

With a quick move around your defender, you drive to the basket. Another defender steps in to block your shot, so you shuffle a pass off to your open teammate. What a play!

1

TIGHT DEFENSE

The game's tied with less than a minute to go. Your knees are bent, ready to match each of your opponent's steps. Your eyes are on the ball as you wait for him to make a move.

SHOT BLOCKER

A player from the other team goes up for a shot, but you are ready for him. You jump and extend your arm, reaching for the basketball. Your entire palm covers the ball for a successful block. Rejected!

1

DOUBLE-TEAMED

You've lit up the scoreboard all game, and the other players have their eyes on you. As soon as you receive a pass, another defender runs over. You secure the ball with both hands and look to pass.

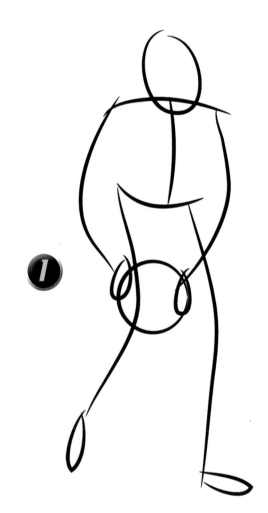

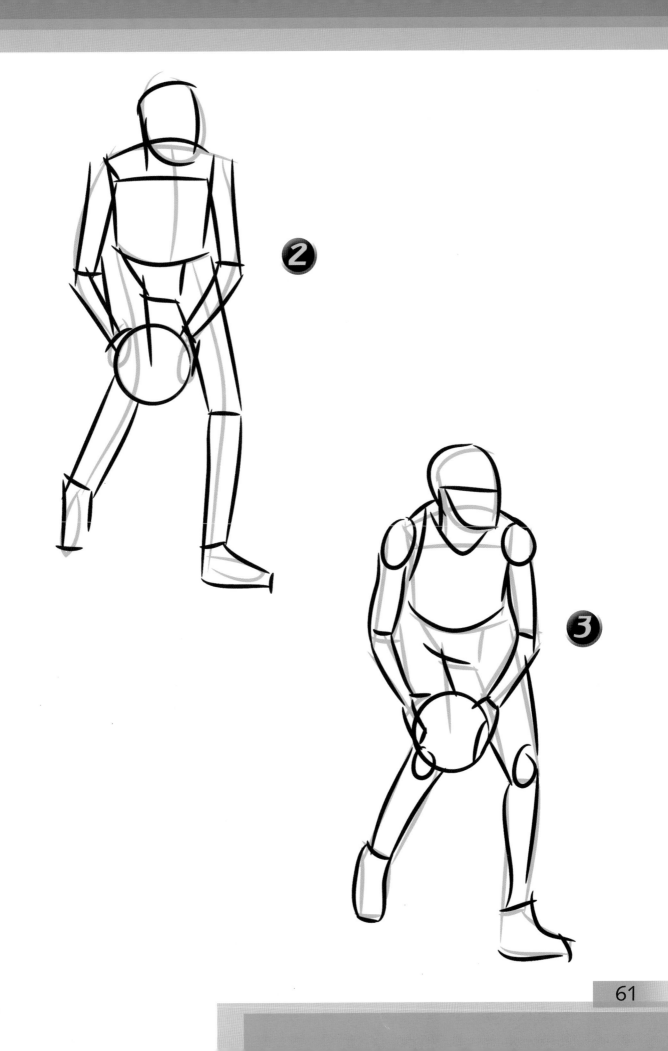

Read More

Ames, Lee J. *Draw 50 Athletes: The Step-by-Step Way to Draw Wrestlers and Figure Skaters, Baseball and Football Players, and Many More.* 2nd ed. New York: Watson-Guptill, 2012.

Omoth, Tyler. *The Ultimate Collection of Pro Basketball Records.* Sports Illustrated Kids. Mankato, Minn.: Capstone Press, 2012.

Slade, Suzanne. *Basketball: How It Works.* Sports Illustrated Kids. Mankato, Minn.: Capstone Press, 2010.

Internet Sites

FactHound offers a safe, fun way to find Internet sites related to this book. All of the sites on FactHound have been researched by our staff.

Here's all you do:

Visit *www.facthound.com*

Type in this code: 9781476531076

Drawing with Sports Illustrated Kids is published by Capstone Press, 1710 Roe Crest Drive, North Mankato, Minnesota 56003
www.capstonepub.com

Copyright © 2014 by Capstone Press, a Capstone imprint. All rights reserved. No part of this publication may be reproduced in whole or in part, or stored in a retrieval system, or transmitted in any form or by any means, electronic, mechanical, photocopying, recording, or otherwise, without written permission of the publisher.

Library of Congress Cataloging-in-Publication Data
Cataloging-in-publication information is on file with the Library of Congress.
ISBN 978-1-4765-3107-6 (library binding)

Check out projects, games and lots more at
www.capstonekids.com

Titles in This Series:

A Baseball Drawing Book

A Basketball Drawing Book

A Hockey Drawing Book

A Football Drawing Book

Editorial Credits
Anthony Wacholtz, editor; Tracy Davies McCabe, designer; Eric Gohl, media researcher; Eric Manske, production specialist

Photo Credits
Sports Illustrated: Al Tielemans, 7, 43, 47, 55, 59, Bill Frakes, 35, 63, Bob Rosato, cover, 23, Damian Strohmeyer, 15, 31, John W. McDonough, 11, 19, 27, 39, 51

Printed in the United States of America in North Mankato, Minnesota.
032013   007223CGF13